LIFE WISDOM

QUOTES FROM

BILLY GRAHAM

A LEGACY OF FAITH

Copyright © 2013 Meadow's Edge Group LLC
978-1-4336-8157-8
Published by B&H Publishing Group, Nashville, Tennessee

Dewey Decimal Classification: B
SUBHD: GRAHAM, BILLY \ CLERGY–BIOGRAPHY \ BAPTISTS–BIOGRAPHY
Publishing Category: Christian Living/Spiritual Growth/Inspiration

CONTENT FOR THIS BOOK WAS GLEANED FROM THE FOLLOWING SOURCES:

Interview with Billy Graham, by Todd Hafer, conducted
during August and September of 1992.

The Leadership Secrets of Billy Graham [now out of print], by Harold
Myra and Marshall Shelley. Used by permission of *Christianity
Today.* See "Acknowledgements" section for more information.

For Your Confirmation: Promises and Prayers [now out of print], Todd
Hafer, editor. Published in 2009 by Gift Books from Hallmark.

Just as I Am: The Autobiography of Billy Graham, copyright © 1997
by Billy Graham. Used by permission of Zondervan. www.zondervan.com

A Legacy of Faith: Things I Learned from My Father by Ruth Graham, ©2006
by Ruth Graham. Used by permission of Zondervan. www.zondervan.com

Press conferences and public addresses.

Packager Development: Meadow's Edge Group LLC
Editorial Development: Todd Hafer
Designed by ThinkpenDesign.com

1 2 3 4 5 6 7 8 9 • 18 17 16 15 14 13

LIFE WISDOM

BILLY GRAHAM

A LEGACY OF FAITH

PUBLISHING GROUP
Nashville, Tennessee

INTRODUCTION

Billy Graham. A spiritual confidant to U.S. Presidents since the days of Harry Truman. A respected adviser to a myriad of world figures, from Winston Churchill to Boris Yeltsin to Ronald Reagan to U2's Bono. For more than seven decades, Mr. Graham spoke to hundreds of millions of people in more than 185 countries and territories—from massive crusades in major cities to small gatherings in remote African villages. He has been a fixture on the Gallup organization's "Ten Most Admired Men in the World" poll, appearing on that list more than fifty times. He has also received the Congressional Gold Medal, and he was honored by the George Washington Carver Memorial Institute for his contribution to race relations.

Well into his 90s, Billy Graham continued to proclaim his message of hope, encouragement, and faith, via televised crusades, a worldwide radio ministry, an internationally syndicated newspaper column, and appearances on programs like Larry King Live.

Mr. Graham is also the author of more than thirty books, including several *New York Times* best sellers.

Raised on a North Carolina dairy farm during the Great Depression, Billy Graham has maintained a humble spirit and singular goal throughout his long ministry: "My purpose in life," he says, "is to help people find a personal relationship with God."

This book features highlights from Mr. Graham's life and ministry. You'll discover stirring quotes, fascinating anecdotes, and profound spiritual insights sure to capture the mind and the heart.

We hope and pray that this book will give you new insights into a remarkable man—and that his wise words will inspire and encourage you and draw you closer to the God whom Billy Graham has served so faithfully.

*"Go into all the world
and preach the gospel to
the whole creation."*

MARK 16:15

THE HEART OF THE
BILLY GRAHAM MESSAGE

I am eager to preach the good news.

Romans 1:15

I recall an old Methodist preacher who came to Harringay Arena in London in 1954. "I have come here every night for ninety-three nights," he told us, "and I have heard only one message." He meant it as a compliment; for he knew as I did that there is **ONLY ONE** Christian message.

God created us in His image. He created us and LOVES *us so that we may live in harmony and fellowship* WITH HIM. *We are not here by chance. God* PUT US HERE *for a* PURPOSE, *and our lives are never fulfilled and complete until His purpose becomes the* FOUNDATION *and center of our lives.*

God provided **HIS LOVE** on the cross. When Christ hung, bled, and died, it was God saying to the world, **"I LOVE YOU."**

God WILL NOT *reject a heart that's broken and sorry for sin. He's not waiting to condemn you, to judge you. He's waiting to* KISS YOU *and say "I love you."*

In God's economy, a person must go down into the valley of grief before he or she can scale the HEIGHTS *of spiritual glory. . . . One must come to the end of "self" before one can really begin to* LIVE.

Unless the soul
is **FED** and
EXERCISED daily,
it becomes weak
and shriveled.
It remains
discontented,
confused, restless.

Tears shed for self are tears of weakness, but tears shed **FOR OTHERS** are a sign of **STRENGTH.**

If a person gets his ATTITUDE *toward money straight, it will help* STRAIGHTEN OUT *almost any other area of his life.*

One of the greatest tenets of the Christian faith is **LOVE**, and love is an **ACTIVE WORD**. We are to go **OUT OF OUR WAY** to love people who perhaps we don't like or who have different skin color or a different ethnic background.

God has given us
TWO HANDS, *one to*
RECEIVE *with and the*
other to GIVE *with.*

HOPE *is both biologically and psychologically* VITAL. *Men and women* MUST *have hope.*

(Speaking after the Oklahoma City bombing)

Times like this will do one of two things: They will either make us hard and bitter and angry at God, or they will make us **TENDER** and **OPEN** and help us to reach out in **TRUST** and **FAITH**. I pray that you will not let bitterness and poison creep into your souls, but that you will **TURN IN FAITH** and **TRUST IN GOD**, even if we cannot understand.

ON FRIENDS AND FAMILY

Show family affection to one another with brotherly love.

ROMANS 12:10

In my ministry, I've been blessed by the people who have surrounded me and worked with me. Without men like Cliff Barrows, Bev Shea, T. W. Wilson, Bill Brown, Guy Martin, Allan Emery, and George Bennett—and all the other people who have served on our board and worked on the crusades— our ministry would be nothing. You would have never heard of me. I give all the credit and glory on this earth to them. And ALL THE GLORY we give collectively to GOD, because without His Holy Spirit, we couldn't have done it.

Everybody needs some friends around him who will say, "You are wrong!" And that includes me. I really value the **FRIENDSHIP** of people who'll just tell it to me **LIKE IT IS**, even though I may try to defend my position for a while.

Ruth and I are
HAPPILY *incompatible.*

Given our own family situation, I have only respect and sympathy for the courageous and committed single parents who for a while (or a lifetime) have to carry the burden alone. The secret of Ruth's survival was in her **COMMITMENT**—not only her marriage commitment before God or her love for me— but also her ministry commitment of the two of us to the **LORD'S PURPOSE** for our lives together.

I want to say to Ruth, my **DEEPEST LOVE** for a companion that's been with me ever since 1943 as my **WIFE**: I love her with all my heart.

UNITY IN DIVERSITY

Above all, put on love—
the perfect bond of unity.

<small>COLOSSIANS 3:14</small>

Jesus said, "Go ye into ALL THE WORLD *and preach the gospel." He didn't say, "Go into the capitalist countries only." I've been in countries with right-wing dictatorships. I've been in countries that have left-wing dictatorships. But I've tried to* STAY RIGHT *with the* GOSPEL OF CHRIST *and stay out of the various political situations.*

The Bible teaches that we are always to **WORK FOR PEACE** and to **PRAY FOR PEACE**. We are to do everything we can.

I am now aware that the FAMILY OF GOD *contains people of* VARIOUS *ethnological, cultural, class, and denominational* DIFFERENCES. . . . *Within the true church there is a mysterious* UNITY *that overrides all divisive factors. In groups which in my ignorant piousness I formerly "frowned upon," I have found men so* DEDICATED TO CHRIST *and so in love with the truth that I have felt unworthy to be in their presence. . . . Although Christians do not always agree . . . what is most needed in the church today is for us to show an unbelieving world that* WE LOVE ONE ANOTHER.

We have to stand in the **MIDDLE** in order to preach to all people, right and left. I haven't been faithful to my own advice in the past. I will be in the future. I'm not for the left wing or the right wing. I'm for the **WHOLE BIRD**.

I don't believe that we should cut ourselves off from people with whom we disagree. I think we ought to talk to them, try to understand their point of view and let them understand our point of view. I don't think the church ought to have this terrible division in which we don't even speak to each other. I went to the World Council of Churches in New Delhi and I went to the National Association of Evangelicals in Denver. I go to all these different groups because I believe that the church is **BIGGER** than any one little group. God has His people in **MANY PLACES**, and I think we are going to be surprised when we get to heaven to find out who is there and who is not there.

Jesus loves ALL PEOPLE,
NO MATTER WHAT
their ethnic or religious
background is. He is
a GOD OF LOVE.

I think a spirit of hostility is wrong. I believe that we should **LOVE**. Regarding those who criticize me from all points, I have asked God a thousand times, "Lord, give me love for them." I don't believe I can preach with liberty unless **GOD HAS GIVEN** me this love and this **MATTER IS CRUCIFIED** in me, until I can say with all my heart that I do love them and could sit down and talk with them, eat with them, fellowship with them and pray with them—anything!

Satan would like nothing better than to have us stop our ministry and start answering critics, tracking down wretched lies and malicious stories. By GOD'S GRACE *I shall continue to preach the* GOSPEL *of Jesus Christ and not stoop to mudslinging, name-calling, and petty little fights over nonessentials.*

I think the church is going to have to RENEW *itself for a* NEW DAY *and take a* NEW APPROACH *to hold people who made commitments to Christ under various circumstances.*

I'm for **MORALITY**, but morality goes beyond sex to **HUMAN FREEDOM** and **SOCIAL JUSTICE**. Evangelists cannot be closely identified with any particular party. We have to stand in the **MIDDLE** in order to preach to all people. . . .

I have really never been a fighter at heart and do not like to engage in sharp answers. I believe that a SOFT ANSWER *turneth away wrath.*

The one **BADGE** of Christianity is not orthodoxy but **LOVE**.

A MAN AND HIS MISSION

*Good news from a distant land is like
cold water to a parched throat.*

<small>PROVERBS 25:25</small>

All of our work and frail human attempts are nothing without **GOD'S BLESSING**, brought about by **PRAYER** and **TRUST IN HIM**. As we look at the years ahead, I pray that God will **STRENGTHEN US** and that we will **NOT LOSE HEART**. For He "is able to do immeasurably **MORE** than all we **ASK** or **IMAGINE**, according to **HIS POWER** that is at work within us" (Ephesians 3:20 NIV).

The TEST *of a preacher is that his congregation goes away saying not, "What a lovely sermon!" but, "I* WILL *do something."*

The MESSAGE *I preach* HASN'T CHANGED. *Circumstances have changed. Problems have changed, but deep inside man has not changed, and the* GOSPEL *hasn't changed.*

(On conversions at Billy Graham crusades)

In some cases they are not lasting at all. In other cases they are absolutely permanent. In every single country of Africa and South America that we have visited, I have met people who got their start in an encounter with Christ at one of these Crusades and are now serving him as missionaries or social workers or medical people. We believe that this is the work of God, and that in each city we come to, there are people whose **HEARTS** are already **PREPARED** by the Spirit of God. They make a **PROFESSION OF FAITH** and it lasts because **GOD DOES IT**. This happened to me.

I believe in the SOVEREIGNTY *of God. God chooses His* SERVANTS. *I believe that God chose me for this particular task at this moment, but whether it is more successful than the work of others whom you have never heard of, I doubt. I think the most* SUCCESSFUL *people are probably individuals whom we will never hear about until we get to* HEAVEN.

When I first heard myself called an **EVANGELIST**, I resented it. I thought of Elmer Gantry. But I've come to like it. It comes from a Greek word meaning **PROCLAIMER**; an evangelist is a proclaimer of the **GOOD NEWS** that God **LOVES** us and wants to **HELP** us.

I want to give God **ALL THE GLORY** and **ALL THE PRAISE** for what has been accomplished in my life and those of my family and associates. I look forward to the day when I can see Jesus **FACE-TO-FACE** and lay at His feet any honor I've ever received, because **HE DESERVES IT ALL**.

Like it or not, money is an essential part of any ministry, and safeguards must be put in place to avoid abuses or misunderstandings and to handle all finances with INTEGRITY *and* OPENNESS. *Most of our financial support comes from the thousands of people who send contributions to us every month. We have no large foundations behind us, and we are dependent on relatively small gifts to meet our expenses every year.*

I don't put myself up as a prophet or someone whom a nation needs. I would say all the nations need the **PREACHING OF THE GOSPEL**. I am an evangelist. The word evangelist comes from the Greek word keryx, which means **PROCLAIMER**. I am a proclaimer of the message of the Bible. I am not preaching some new idea, some new philosophy, or something I have thought up. I am simply **PREACHING THE BIBLE**, the same old truths that the church has believed for centuries.

Being a CHRISTIAN *is more than just an instantaneous conversion—it is a* DAILY PROCESS *whereby you grow to become* MORE LIKE CHRIST.

When we come to a large city, all the controversies within the church are brought into focus by the Crusade. The tension is not in us; it is already there. There are those who, for one reason or another, feel they cannot support the meetings. I never answer them, I never mention them, I never attack them. I RESPECT their point of view, but we go on PREACHING THE GOSPEL.

The tendency among some evangelists was to exaggerate their successes or to claim higher attendance numbers than they really had. We **COMMITTED** ourselves to **INTEGRITY** in our publicity and our reporting.

If anything has been accomplished through my life, it has been solely GOD'S DOING, *not mine, and* HE—*not I*—*must get the* CREDIT.

When I accepted the call to ministry, I told God I'd go **ANYWHERE** He wanted me to go. I'd go to **HELL** if He'd give me **SAFE CONDUCT OUT**.

Preaching . . . involves us in a **SPIRITUAL BATTLE** with the forces of evil. I am always deeply conscious that I am absolutely helpless and that only the **HOLY SPIRIT** can penetrate the minds and hearts of those who are without Christ. . . . All I am doing is **SOWING A SEED**. It is God—and only God—who can make that seed bear **FRUIT**.

My calling is to preach the LOVE *of God and the* FORGIVENESS *of God and the fact that He* DOES FORGIVE *us. That's what the cross is all about, what the resurrection is all about,* THAT'S THE GOSPEL.

If **ONE PERSON** received Christ as Lord and Savior and had his or her life changed, I feel that our ministry is **WORTHWHILE**, because Jesus said, "What shall it profit a man if he **GAINS** the **WHOLE WORLD** and **LOSES** his **OWN SOUL**?" Well, suppose one soul is saved—that would be **WORTH THE WHOLE WORLD**.

*I pray that the books
I have written will*
ENCOURAGE *the people
who read them and* GIVE
HOPE *to the despairing.*

All of us in Christian ministry need to LIVE *and* WORK *with* INTEGRITY. *By integrity, I mean the* MORAL VALUE *that makes people the same on the inside as they are on the outside— with no discrepancy between what they* SAY *and what they* DO, *between their* WALK *and their* TALK. *In the Old Testament, Solomon wrote, "The man of integrity walks* SECURELY, *but he who takes crooked paths will be found out. Be sure your sins will find you out." We cannot hide. We think we are hiding from the Lord, but we are not.*

God **STILL LOVES** us. He yearns to **FORGIVE** us and **BRING** us back to Himself. He wants to fill our lives with **MEANING** and **PURPOSE** right now. Then He wants us to spend all eternity **WITH HIM** in Heaven, **FREE FOREVER** from the pain and sorrow and death of this world.

You CANNOT *come to Christ with just your mind. You* CAN'T *think your way to Jesus. Solomon had wealth, women, and religion, but* NO PEACE.

THE STATE OF AMERICA . . . AND THE WORLD

For the oppressed will not always be forgotten;
the hope of the afflicted will not perish forever.

PSALM 9:18

Much of the world [continues] feeling the effects of terrorism and war, but there are other things that are bothering us: disease, poverty, racism, hate, loneliness, AIDS, unemployment, divorce, psychological problems, boredom, murder statistics—the world DIDN'T STOP *sinning or getting bored after September 11. We know that* SOMETHING IS WRONG *with human nature.* SIN *is what's wrong with the world, and* ONLY JESUS CHRIST *can* SOLVE *it.*

In a world of greed, where materialistic values often take first place, pleasure has become a god—and a great premium is placed on cleverness—our **GREATEST NEED** is **MORAL INTEGRITY**. Job said, "Till I die, **I WILL NOT DENY** my integrity." David, the great king of Israel, wrote, "**I WILL WALK** in mine integrity."

I believe that if this nation of ours would TURN TO GOD *in* PRAYER *and in* FAITH, *and would* LIVE *the Christian life, God would hear from heaven. There is no telling how greatly this nation could* LEAD THE WORLD *if we were living the way God would have us to live.*

Christians have often been **TOO STRIDENT** and **LEGALISTIC**.

I don't think we will have **PERMANENT PEACE** in the world as long as man's heart stays as it is—as long as there is hate and jealousy and greed and lust. You **CANNOT HAVE PEACE** when **MAN'S HEART IS NOT AT PEACE.**

[With each new decade], I believe America has gone a long way down the wrong road. We must CHANGE ROADS, TURN AROUND, *and* GO BACK. *We must* REPENT *and* COMMIT *our lives to God and to the moral and spiritual principles that have made this nation great, and translate that commitment into* ACTION *in our homes, neighborhoods, and our society.*

Human nature is the same the world over, and when the gospel of Christ is preached in **SIMPLICITY** and **POWER**, there is a **RESPONSE** in the human soul.

The deepest problems of the human race are SPIRITUAL. *They are rooted in man's refusal to seek God's way for his life. The problem is the human heart, which* GOD ALONE CAN CHANGE.

(Responding to the events of September 11, 2001)

[The following words are from a statement Billy Graham issued just after the terrorist attacks of September 11—and from an address he gave at an interfaith service held at the National Cathedral in Washington, just three days after the attacks.]

In times like these, we realize how weak and inadequate we are, and our greatest need is to **TURN** in **REPENTANCE** and **FAITH** to the God of all **MERCY** and the Father of all **COMFORT**. If ever there was a time for us to **TURN TO GOD** and to **PRAY AS A NATION**, it is **NOW**, that this evil will spread no further. It is also a time for us to remember the words of the psalmist: "God is our **REFUGE** and **STRENGTH**, a very present help in trouble."

We come together today to **AFFIRM** our conviction that God **CARES** about us, whatever our ethnic, religious, or political background may be. The Bible says that He is the "God of **ALL COMFORT**, who comforts us in all our troubles. . . ."

But today, we especially come together in this service to **CONFESS** our need of God. We've **ALWAYS NEEDED** God from the beginning of this nation, but today we need Him especially. We're facing a new kind of enemy. We're involved in a new kind of warfare, and we **NEED THE HELP** of the Spirit of God. The Bible's words are our **HOPE**: "God is our **REFUGE** and **STRENGTH**, a very present **HELP** in trouble. Therefore we will not fear, though the earth give way and the mountains fall in to the heart of the sea."

But how do we understand something like this? Why does God allow evil like this to take place? Perhaps that is what you are asking now. You may even be angry at God. I want to assure you that God **UNDERSTANDS** these feelings that you may have. . . . **GOD CAN BE TRUSTED**, even when life seems darkest. But what are some of the **LESSONS** we can **LEARN**?

First, we are reminded of the mystery and reality of evil. I have been asked hundreds of times in my life why God allows tragedy and suffering. I have to confess that I really don't know the answer totally, even to my own satisfaction. I have to **ACCEPT BY FAITH** that God is **SOVEREIGN**, and He's a God of **LOVE** and **MERCY** and **COMPASSION** in the midst of suffering. . . .

The lesson about this event is not only about the mystery of iniquity and evil, but, secondly, it's a lesson about our **NEED** for **EACH OTHER.** What an example New York and Washington have been to the world these past few days! None of us will ever forget the pictures of our courageous firefighters and police, many of whom have lost friends and colleagues, or the hundreds of people attending or standing patiently in line to donate blood. A tragedy like this could have torn our country apart, but instead it has **UNITED** us and we've become a **FAMILY.** . . . We are **MORE UNITED** than **EVER BEFORE**.

Finally, difficult as it may be for us to see right now—this event can give a **MESSAGE OF HOPE**—hope for the **PRESENT**, and hope for the **FUTURE**.

Yes, **THERE IS HOPE**. There is hope for the present because I believe the stage has already been set for a **NEW SPIRIT** in our nation. One of the things we desperately need is a **SPIRITUAL RENEWAL** in this country. . . . And God has told us in His Word, time after time, that we are to **REPENT** of our sins and we're to **TURN** to Him and He will **BLESS** us in a **NEW WAY**.

But there is also a **HOPE** for the **FUTURE**, because of God's **PROMISES**. As a Christian, I have hope, not just for this life, but for **HEAVEN** and the **LIFE TO COME**. And many of those people who died this past week are in heaven right now, and they wouldn't want to come back. It's so **GLORIOUS** and **WONDERFUL**. And that's the hope for all of us who put our **FAITH** in God. I pray that you will have this hope in your heart.

This event reminds us of the brevity and uncertainty of life. We never know when we, too, will be called into eternity. . . . And that's why each of us needs to **FACE** our own **SPIRITUAL NEED** and **COMMIT** ourselves to **GOD** and **HIS WILL** now.

Here in this majestic National Cathedral, we see all around us the symbols of the **CROSS**. The Cross tells us that God **UNDERSTANDS** our sins and our suffering, for He took upon himself, in the person of Jesus Christ, our sins and our suffering. And from the Cross, God declares, "**I LOVE YOU.** I know the heartaches and the sorrows and the pains that you feel. **BUT I LOVE YOU.**"

The story does not end with the Cross, for Easter points us **BEYOND** the tragedy of the Cross to the empty tomb. It tells us that there is **HOPE** for **ETERNAL LIFE,** for Christ has **CONQUERED** evil and death, and hell. Yes, **THERE IS HOPE.**

I've become an old man now, and I've preached all over the world, and the older I get, the more I **CLING** to that **HOPE** that I started with many years ago and proclaimed in many languages to many parts of the world. . . .

This has been a terrible week, with many tears, but it also has been a week of **GREAT FAITH**. My prayer today is that we will feel the **LOVING ARMS** of God wrapped around us, and will know in our hearts that He will **NEVER FORSAKE** us as we **TRUST** in Him.

May God **BLESS** you all.

(Speaking in South Africa)

CHRISTIANITY *is not a white man's religion, and don't let anybody ever tell you that it's white or black.* CHRIST BELONGS *to* ALL PEOPLE!

As long as there is one man in the world who hates another man because of the color of his skin or the shape of his nose or for some other reason, you have the possibility of war—As long as you have men in the world greedy for power, there is potential conflict. I believe that the **GOSPEL OF CHRIST** is the **ONLY POWER** in the world that can **TRANSFORM** the heart of man and make it **LOVE** instead of hate. But will the whole world come to Christ? The Bible teaches otherwise, in my opinion.

We all live under GRACE
and do the best we can.

PERSONAL REVELATIONS

So I take pleasure in weaknesses,
insults, catastrophes, persecutions,
and in pressures, because of Christ.
For when I am weak, then I am strong.

2 Corinthians 12:10

Often, when I have an opportunity to visit world leaders, I go as a FRIEND. *I don't counsel world leaders on public affairs. In fact, I'm not asked questions about how this particular thing or [another] should be run. We talk about* FAITH, *we talk about* SPIRITUAL MATTERS, *and, occasionally, we talk about our* FAMILIES.

(On enduring Parkinson's disease)

Suffering is part of the human condition, and it comes to us all. The **KEY** is how we **REACT** to it, either turning away from God in anger and bitterness or **GROWING CLOSER** to Him in **TRUST** and **CONFIDENCE**.

God can be TRUSTED,
*even when life seems at its
darkest. From the cross, God
declares,* "I LOVE YOU.
*I know the heartaches and
the sorrows and the pains
you feel, but I love* YOU."

I am very happy when people come in large numbers, but I have also conditioned myself to preaching to many empty seats. God often does His **GREATEST WORK** when the audience is **SMALL**. Christ spent at least half his time with just a **HANDFUL** of people and preached His **GREATEST SERMON** to **ONE** person [Nicodemus].

If I convert any, they won't be real conversions. The **LORD** has to do the **CONVERTING**. The records of the true converts, I believe, are kept in **HEAVEN**. No one will know the answer . . . until we stand before God on the judgment day.

I am thankful for the PEACE *of God in my heart, and that could happen to everybody—whatever your problem, whatever your need,* JESUS *can come into your heart and* FORGIVE *you and* GUARANTEE *to you* LIFE *in this life, but also life* BEYOND *this life.*

When it comes to the gospel, you be **FAITHFUL** and the **HOLY SPIRIT** will do the **COMMUNICATING** in a way you could never do.

(On his popularity and success)

That's one of the first things I'm going to ask God when I get to heaven, because I don't know. I'm the most ordinary person in the world. I'm amazed at it all. To me, IT'S JUST GOD. *It's the* SOVEREIGNTY *of God in choosing me as He did Jeremiah, or Isaiah.*

I believe EVERY WORD *of the Bible, from Genesis to Revelation, but the Bible isn't a scientific document; it's written for the* COMMON PEOPLE, *in language they can* UNDERSTAND.

These men did evangelists'
work—men like John Wesley,
and Dwight L. Moody,
and William Wilberforce.
We've forgotten today
how the **EVANGELIST** is
as **IMPORTANT** as the
PASTOR and the **TEACHER**.
Of course I'm not worthy to
lick these men's boots . . .
I shouldn't be mentioned.

As I look back over my life, I also have many regrets. I have failed many times, and I would do many things differently. For one thing, I would SPEAK LESS *and* STUDY MORE, *and I would* SPEND MORE TIME *with my* FAMILY. *When I look back over the schedule I kept thirty or forty years ago, I am staggered by all the things we did and the engagements we kept.*

I thought when I started . . . that we could turn the world **UPSIDE DOWN;** that the whole world would turn to God. I am not quite that naive now. Sin is a little blacker than I thought it was; and I am no longer taken in by statistics. They don't tell the **STORY**.

I must admit I feel very inadequate at times when talking about **GOD'S DISCIPLINE** through pain. . . . When those I love have suffered, I have wished I could take their pain **AS MY OWN.**

(Does Billy Graham want to preach all his life?)

I asked myself that question for the umpteenth time [many years ago] on one of my nighttime walks around the golf course. I got down on my knees. Then I prostrated myself on the dewy turf. "O God," I sobbed, "if you want me to serve You, I WILL." The moonlight, the moss, the breeze, the green, the golf course—all the surroundings stayed the same. No sign in the heavens. No voice from above. But IN MY SPIRIT I knew I had been called to the ministry. And I knew my answer was YES.

I'm not a great man. I just have a **GREAT MESSAGE.**

God knows my MOTIVE *and He knows my* HEART, *and God uses even that simple presentation that might have been poorly done, and He* APPLIES *it to the human heart.*

I know my time on earth will not be over until He calls me home. I admit I don't like the burdens of old age—the slow decline in energy, the physical annoyances, the pain of losing loved ones, the sadness of seeing friends decline. But old age can be a SPECIAL TIME *of life, and* God has LESSONS *to* TEACH *us through it. . . . I may not be able to do everything I once did (nor does God expect me to), but I am called to be* FAITHFUL *to what I can do.*

Many a time under my own preaching I've **RECOMMITTED** my life to the Lord, standing there—because we all have moments when we feel that God is speaking in a **VERY SPECIAL WAY** to us . . . and many times I come forward with the people, in my heart, to make a **RECOMMITMENT** in my own life.

God called me to PREACH, *and I do not intend to do anything else as long as I live.*

All that I have been able to do, I owe to **JESUS CHRIST**. I feel I am a **SPECTATOR** watching what **GOD IS DOING**.

I remember a particular incident at the beginning of my ministry. During a 1949 conference in the mountains east of Los Angeles, I had serious doubts about God, Christ, and the Bible. I decided I had to clarify them one way or the other. I had to find PEACE about it all in my own heart . . .

. . . in the moonlight, I went into the woods. I opened the Bible and laid it on a tree stump. Then I knelt down and said, "Oh, God, I don't understand all that is in this book. Many things seem to be contradictory. I cannot intellectually accept it, but I am going to ACCEPT *it by* FAITH *as* YOUR WORD, *your* INSPIRED, DIVINE WORD." *And I did accept it by faith, and I have* NEVER HAD A DOUBT *since then.*

Looking back, I can see how as I was growing up, the people in my hometown, Charlotte, North Carolina, and that city's culture and religious faith helped mold my **CHARACTER** and helped give me the **VALUES** and **SPIRITUAL DEPTH** that I believe are required for the work God called me to do.

(On books that have influenced him.)

First, I would have to say the BIBLE. My wife and I read from the Psalms every day—five Psalms and one chapter of Proverbs. The Psalms teach you how to GET ALONG with GOD; Proverbs teaches you how to GET ALONG with PEOPLE. I also try to read books on current trends and economics. And every day I read a lot of newspapers and news magazines.

LEARNING *was an* INSATIABLE *desire with me. I burned to learn. I am a man still in* PROCESS.

A keen **SENSE OF HUMOR** helps us **OVERLOOK** the unbecoming, **UNDERSTAND** the unconventional, **TOLERATE** the unpleasant, **OVERCOME** the unexpected, and **OUTLAST** the unbearable.

GOD'S LOVE *has* SEEN ME THROUGH *sickness, discouragement, and frustration.* HIS LOVE *has* SUSTAINED *me during times of disappointment and bewilderment.*

The Lord has always arranged my life that I have had to keep **DEPENDENT** on Him. Over and over again, I went to my knees and asked the **SPIRIT OF WISDOM** for **GUIDANCE** and **DIRECTION**. There were times when I was tempted to flee from problems and pressures and my inability to cope with them; but somehow, even in moments of confusion and indecision, it seemed I could trace the steady hand of God's **SOVEREIGNTY** leading me on.

Every day I have to **RENEW** my heart before God and ask for His **GRACE** and **STRENGTH.**

I take time EACH DAY *in the morning and evening to* READ *passages of Scripture and ask the Lord to* SPEAK *to me through them—apart from any preparations of sermon material.*

I believe there is a **WORLDWIDE HUNGER** for God.

I want people to call me BILLY—not Reverend William F. Graham— so that they will feel that they can come to me with any of their problems or needs.

THE POWER OF PRAYER

*The LORD has heard my plea for help;
the LORD accepts my prayer.*

PSALM 6:9

PRAYER *is not just asking. It is* LISTENING *for God's orders.*

I have learned, I believe, to "pray **WITHOUT CEASING**." I find myself constantly in **PRAYER** and **FELLOWSHIP** with God, even while I am talking to other people or doing other things.

Every time my mother prayed with one of us, and every time my parents prayed for their sons and daughters, they were DECLARING *their* DEPENDENCE *on God for the* WISDOM *and* STRENGTH *and* COURAGE *to stay in control of life,* NO MATTER *what circumstances might bring.*

We know we cannot do **EVERYTHING** that needs to be done, but in a world that is never free of turmoil, Christ calls us to do **WHAT WE CAN.**

God wants us to have **COMPASSION** on those who are suffering and **DO WHAT WE CAN** to **HELP.**

FAITH, *more than fighting, can* CHANGE *the course of events today. United, believing, self-humbling, God-exalting* PRAYER *now can change the course of* HISTORY.

QUOTABLE QUIPS

He said to me, "Son of man, stand up on your feet and I will speak with you."

Ezekiel 2:1

When wealth is lost, nothing is lost. When health is lost, something is lost. When **CHARACTER** is lost, **EVERYTHING** is lost.

Hot HEADS *and cold* HEARTS *never solved anything.*

COURAGE is contagious. When a **BRAVE MAN** takes a stand, the spines of **OTHERS** are stiffened.

*When we come
to the END
of ourselves,
we come to the
BEGINNING
of God.*

The only HOPE *for enduring* PEACE *is Jesus Christ.*

The **ONLY TIME** my prayers are never answered is on the **GOLF COURSE**.

I am selling the GREATEST *product in the world. Why shouldn't it be* PROMOTED *as well as* SOAP?

There is nothing wrong with men possessing riches. The **WRONG** comes when **RICHES** possess **MEN.**

Mountaintops are for VIEWS *and* INSPIRATION, *but fruit is grown in the* VALLEYS.

CONFRONTING SOCIAL INJUSTICE

The LORD is a refuge for the oppressed,
a refuge in times of trouble.

PSALM 9:9

Much of my life has been a PILGRIMAGE—*constantly learning, changing, growing, and maturing. I have come to see in* DEEPER *ways some of the implications of my faith and message, not the least of which is the area of human rights and racial and ethnic understanding.*

"You're going the **WRONG WAY**, sister. **ALL THE CHILDREN** belong down front so God can **SMILE** on them."

[Billy Graham to a young African-American girl who was being ushered by a white woman to a segregated area in the back of a tent revival in the early 1940s.]

Bigotry of
ANY KIND *is*
a SIN *in*
GOD'S EYES.

I think it is very evident that Moses had an Ethiopian wife whose skin was dark. I don't think that **CHRIST'S SKIN** was as light as mine, or perhaps as dark as the West African's. He was born in a part of the world where his skin was probably more of a brown or swarthy color. To base racial segregation on the Bible, I think, is **RIDICULOUS**. Of course you can make the Bible prove anything. You can twist the Scripture all around and take verses and chapters out of context, but the Bible teaches that we are **RIGHTLY** to divide the Word of truth, and that we are to do it with spiritual **DISCERNMENT**. I just **CANNOT FIND ANYTHING** to substantiate racial barriers and differences in the Bible.

I believe that Christians are to have **SOCIAL CONCERN** and that every Christian should be interested in the **MORAL** and **SPIRITUAL** betterment of his community.

Christ said, "By THIS *shall all men know that ye are my disciples, if ye have* LOVE ONE TO ANOTHER." *This affects the* CHURCH, *it affects* RACE, *it affects* ALL SORTS *of areas of life.*

There is no scriptural basis for segregation. The ground at the foot of the **CROSS** is **LEVEL**, and it touches my heart when I see whites standing **SHOULDER TO SHOULDER** with blacks at the cross.

It has become a byword that the MOST SEGREGATED *hour of the week is still* ELEVEN O'CLOCK *Sunday morning.*

Racial prejudice, anti-Semitism, or hatred of anyone with different beliefs has NO PLACE *in the human mind or heart. I urge everyone to* EXAMINE *themselves and* RENEW *their own hearts before God. Only the* SUPERNATURAL LOVE *of God through changed lives can* SOLVE *the problems that we face in our world.*

Hatred and racism
are fundamentally
MORAL and **SPIRITUAL**
problems.

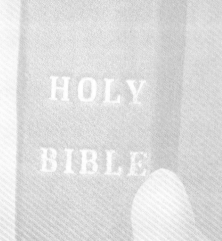

FACING THE FUTURE

I have spoken; yes, I have called him;
I have brought him, and he
will succeed in his mission.

Isaiah 48:15

The older I get, the more I am asked who will succeed me. Well, the fact is that I am just ONE *of many* THOUSANDS *who have been called to be an* EVANGELIST. *I don't need a successor, only* WILLING HANDS *to accept the torch I have been carrying.*

It is time for the church to use technology to make a **STATEMENT** that in the midst of chaos, emptiness, and despair, there is **HOPE** in the person of **JESUS CHRIST**.

The message of the gospel NEVER CHANGES—*and for good reason:* GOD *never changes, and neither does our basic* SPIRITUAL NEED, *nor His* ANSWER *to that need. But the methods of presenting the message do change. In fact, they must change if we are to* KEEP PACE *with a changing world. If we fail to* BRIDGE THE GAP *between us and those we hope to reach, our message will not be communicated, and our efforts will be in vain.*

The **DESTINY** of men and nations is always being decided. Every generation is **CRUCIAL**; every generation is **STRATEGIC**. But we are not responsible for the past generation, and we cannot bear full responsibility for the next one. However, we do have **OUR GENERATION**! God will hold us **RESPONSIBLE** . . . for how well we fulfilled our **RESPONSIBILITIES** and took advantage of **OPPORTUNITIES**.

God called me to **PREACH**, and I will never do anything else as long as I live. I believe I have a **CALLING** from God and a **COMMAND** from Christ to go to the **WHOLE WORLD**.

The more I get OLDER, *the more I get* CLOSER *to death, the* HAPPIER *I am. I am filled with* ANTICIPATION—*I'm looking forward to it. One reason is I'll get some* REST!

What is **HEAVEN** going to be like? There is a **MYSTERY** to heaven. Yet I believe the Bible teaches that heaven is a literal place. Is it one of the stars? I don't know. I can't even **SPECULATE**. The Bible doesn't inform us. I believe that out there in space, where there are one-thousand-million galaxies, each a hundred thousand light years or more in diameter, God can find some place to put us in heaven. I'm not worried about where it is. I know it is going to be **WHERE JESUS IS.** Christians don't have to go around discouraged . . . with their shoulders bent. Think of it—the **JOY**, the **PEACE**, the sense of **FORGIVENESS** that He gives you, and then heaven too.

I might step aside from the organization, because it gets beyond me sometimes, but I won't retire from PREACHING. *We have a lot of little churches around my home in the mountains of North Carolina. They will take me, and I can go there and preach until the day the Lord calls me to* HEAVEN. *I was* CALLED BY GOD *to do this, and I don't read anyplace in the Bible where any of His servants* RETIRED.

I look forward to HEAVEN. . . . *I also look forward to* SERVING *God in ways we can't begin to imagine, for the Bible makes it clear that Heaven is not a place of idleness. And most of all, I look forward to* SEEING CHRIST *and* BOWING *before Him in* PRAISE *and* GRATITUDE *for all He has done for us.*

No, I don't know the **FUTURE,** but I do know this: **THE BEST IS YET TO BE**! Heaven **AWAITS** us. . . . This is the **HOPE** of every believer. It is **MY HOPE**, and I pray that it is **YOUR HOPE** as well. I know that soon my life will be over. **I THANK GOD** for it, and for all He has given me in this life.

(From a 2005 press conference at Rockefeller Center)

I'm glad that at the end of it all the Bible says that Jesus is COMING BACK *to this earth, and someday He is going to* REIGN, *and there'll be* NO TEARS, NO SUFFERING, *no* DEATH . . . *a* WONDERFUL *future; and I hope I'll meet all of you there. Bring your* CAMERA, *because I may have one too!"*

I've read the **LAST PAGE** of the **BIBLE**. It's all going to turn out **ALL RIGHT**.

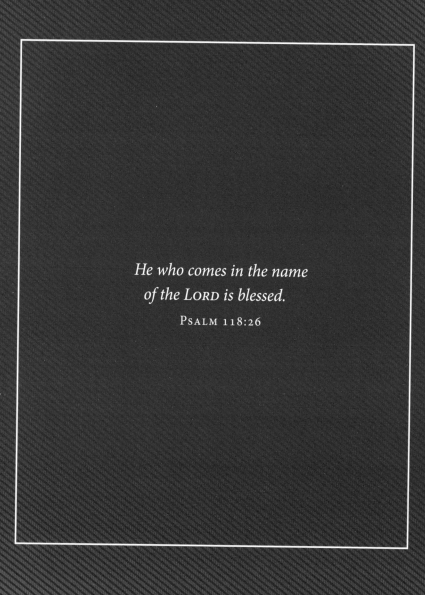

*He who comes in the name
of the LORD is blessed.*

PSALM 118:26

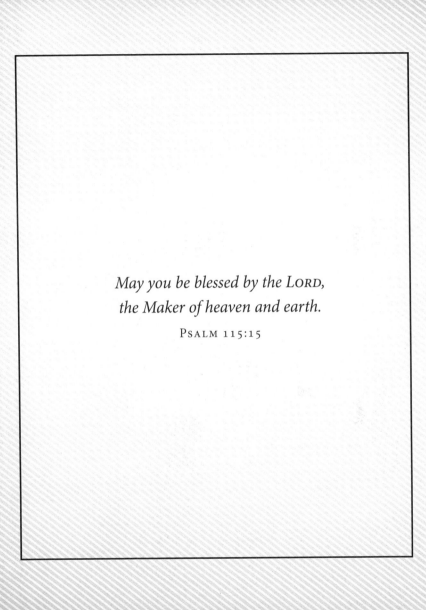

May you be blessed by the LORD,
the Maker of heaven and earth.

PSALM 115:15

ACKNOWLEDGMENTS

Thank you, Seamus Dillon and Marshall Shelley
for helping make this book possible. Your
kindness and graciousness are exemplary.

Grateful acknowledgement is also due *The Quote Verifier: Who
Said What, Where, and When* by Ralph Keyes. 2006, St. Martin's
Press. This reference has proved to be a vital source for quote
attribution and accuracy, on this and many other books.

The quotes from the book *The Leadership Secrets of Billy
Graham* are found on the following pages: 16–17, 19, 28,
34, 41, 43, 47, 57, 59, 71, 98,108, 110–111, 114, 120–122,
130, 138–140, 144–146, 154, 160–161, and 171. For
more information on this book, see the copyright page.

If you enjoyed reading this book and would like to share its impact on your life, we would like to hear from you. Please send your comments via email to: meadowsedgegroup@gmail.com or write us at:

Meadow's Edge Group
P.O. Box 6947
Siloam Springs, AR 72761

Also available:

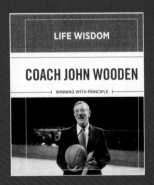

LIFE WISDOM

COACH JOHN WOODEN

WINNING WITH PRINCIPLE

Both Life Wisdom books are available at bookstores everywhere or go to www.BHPublishingGroup.com for further information.